# Now That I'm a Christian

MW00990327

## By R. B. Sweet

## CONTENTS

© 1948 by R. B. Sweet

Revision © 1991, 1996, 2003 by Sweet Publishing, PO Box 55127, Fort Worth, Texas 76054. All rights reserved.

Unless otherwise identified, all Scripture references are from the Holy Bible, New International Version © 1973 1978, 1984 by the International Bible Society; used by permission of Zondervan Bible Publishers.

Scripture references marked KJV are from the King James Version of the Bible.

Printed in the United States. All rights reserved.

03  04  05  06  07  08  09  10  *  20  19  18  17

# Certificate of Baptism

By the grace of God,

I _Earline (Tiny) Brown,_

became a Christian by being baptized

as a demonstration and confession of

my faith in Jesus Christ and for the

forgiveness of my sins on the

_13_ day of _October_ , _2013_ , at

_Highland Acres Church of Christ_

(place)

Assisted by

_David Lockhart_

# Now That I'm a Christian

I am a part of a loving family, or fellowship—the body of Christ.

> *You have come to God, the judge of all men, to the spirits of righteous men made perfect.*
>
> Hebrews 12:23

My family has been "called out" from the world to show God's love and mercy to everyone.

> *But you are a chosen people, a royal priesthood, a holy nation, a people belonging to God, that you may declare the praises of him who called you out of darkness into his wonderful light. Once you were not a people, but now you are the people of God; once you had not received mercy, but now you have received mercy.*
>
> 1 Peter 2:9–10

And now we have compelling reasons to live righteously and godly.

> *For the grace of God that brings salvation has appeared to all men. It teaches us to say "No" to ungodliness and worldly passions, and to live self-controlled, upright and godly lives in this present age, while we wait for the blessed hope—the glorious appearing of our great God and Savior, Jesus Christ, who gave himself for us to redeem us from all wickedness and to purify for himself a people that are his very own, eager to do what is good.*
>
> Titus 2:11–14

Since this is true, I want to be an active part of this family and to promote its good.

*As a prisoner for the Lord, then, I urge you to live a life worthy of the calling you have received. Be completely humble and gentle; be patient, bearing with one another in love. Make every effort to keep the unity of the Spirit through the bond of peace.*
Ephesians 4:1–3

I also want to ensure my own spiritual development.

*Until we all reach unity in the faith and in the knowledge of the Son of God and become mature, attaining to the whole measure of the fullness of Christ.*
Ephesians 4:13

In order to do this, I will study the Bible daily to understand its message as it applies to my own life.

*Do your best to present yourself to God as one approved, a workman who does not need to be ashamed and who correctly handles the word of truth.*
2 Timothy 2:15

To reaffirm my salvation, and so that I can help others, I will review the way I became a Christian so that I can be ready to give a reason for my hope to my friends and family when they ask.

*But in your hearts set apart Christ as Lord. Always be prepared to give an answer to everyone who asks you to give the reason for the hope that you have. But do this with gentleness and respect.*
1 Peter 3:15

First, I learned that I am a sinner.

*For all have sinned and fall short of the glory of God.*
Romans 3:23

I learned this by hearing God's Word.

*For since in the wisdom of God the world through its wisdom did not know him, God was pleased through the foolishness of what was preached to save those who believe.*

1 Corinthians 1:21

Through the study of the Scriptures, I learned that faith in God is necessary.

*And without faith it is impossible to please God, because anyone who comes to him must believe that he exists and that he rewards those who earnestly seek him.*

Hebrews 11:6

Faith in Jesus as the Christ, the Savior, the Son of God is also part of my saving faith. Jesus said . . .

*"Do not let your hearts be troubled. Trust in God; trust also in me."*

John 14:1

*You are all sons of God through faith in Christ Jesus.*

Galatians 3:26

My faith in God developed through a careful consideration of such thoughts as this:

*The heavens declare the glory of God; the skies proclaim the work of his hands.*

Psalm 19:1

My faith in Jesus as the Christ came by knowing this:

*Jesus did many other miraculous signs in the presence of his disciples, which are not recorded in this book. But these are written that you may believe that Jesus is the Christ, the Son of God, and that by believing you may have life in his name.*

John 20:30–31

*We did not follow cleverly invented stories when we told you about the power and coming of our Lord Jesus Christ, but we were eyewitnesses of his majesty. For he received honor and glory from God the Father when the voice came to him from the Majestic Glory, saying, "This is my Son, whom I love; with him I am well pleased." We ourselves heard this voice that came from heaven when we were with him on the sacred mountain.*

*And we have the word of the prophets made more certain, and you will do well to pay attention to it, as a light shining in a dark place, until the day dawns and the morning star rises in your hearts. Above all, you must understand that no prophecy of Scripture came about by the prophet's own interpretation. For prophecy never had its origin in the will of man, but men spoke from God as they were carried along by the Holy Spirit.*

2 Peter 1:16–21

I learned that I need to change the way I live; that is, I repented of my love of evil and my sinful ways.

Jesus said:

*I tell you, no! But unless you repent, you too will all perish.* Luke 13:3

Peter said:

*Repent, then, and turn to God, so that your sins may be wiped out, that times of refreshing may come from the Lord.* Acts 3:19

Paul said:

*In the past God overlooked such ignorance, but now he commands all people everywhere to repent. For he has set a day when he will judge the world with justice by the man he has appointed. He has given proof of this to all men by raising him from the dead.*

Acts 17:30–31

The first thing I did to show my confidence in Christ was to confess in front of others that He is the Son of God:

*Whoever acknowledges me before men, I will also acknowledge him before my Father in heaven.*

Matthew 10:32

*But what does it say? "The word is near you; it is in your mouth and in your heart," that is, the word of faith we are proclaiming: That if you confess with your mouth, "Jesus is Lord," and believe in your heart that God raised him from the dead, you will be saved. For it is with your heart that you believe and are justified, and it is with your mouth that you confess and are saved.*

Romans 10:8–10

The New Testament also taught me to confess Jesus as Lord. There is no other verbal or public confession. And yet, that confession alone is not enough, for I also learned this:

*Therefore, since we have a great high priest who has gone through the heavens, Jesus the Son of God, let us hold firmly to the faith we profess.*

Hebrews 4:14

With that preparation, I was baptized.

*Peter replied, "Repent and be baptized, every one of you, in the name of Jesus Christ for the forgiveness of your sins. And you will receive the gift of the Holy Spirit.*

Acts 2:38

And I began my life as a child of God.

*We died to sin; how can we live in it any longer? Or don't you know that all of us who were baptized into Christ Jesus were baptized into his death? We were therefore buried with him through baptism into death in order that, just as Christ was raised from the dead through the glory of the Father, we too may live a new life.*

Romans 6:2–4

7

That baptism put me into Christ.

*For all of you who were baptized into Christ have clothed yourselves with Christ.*

Galatians 3:27

Baptism identified me with Christ and his death because it is a burial and a resurrection. I found also that baptism is intended for believers—persons who are old enough to have faith in Christ and to make confession of their faith. Jesus' last directions to his apostles teach this. We call those last words The Great Commission.

*Then Jesus came to them and said, "All authority in heaven and on earth has been given to me. Therefore go and make disciples of all nations, baptizing them in the name of the Father and of the Son and of the Holy Spirit, and teaching them to obey everything I have commanded you. And surely I am with you always, to the very end of the age."*

Matthew 28:18-20

*He said to them, "Go into all the world and preach the good news to all creation. Whoever believes and is baptized will be saved, but whoever does not believe will be condemned."*

Mark 16:15, 16

*He told them, "This is what is written: The Christ will suffer and rise from the dead on the third day, and repentance and forgiveness of sins will be preached in his name to all nations, beginning at Jerusalem. You are witnesses of these things."*

Luke 24:46–48

When the apostles began preaching as Jesus had told them to do, here's what happened:

*When the people heard this, they were cut to the heart and said to Peter and the other apostles, "Brothers, what shall we do?"*

*Peter replied, "Repent and be baptized, every one of you, in the name of Jesus Christ for the forgiveness of your sins. And you will receive the gift of the Holy Spirit. The promise is for you and your children and for all who are far off—for all whom the Lord our God will call."*

*With many other words he warned them; and he pleaded with them, "Save yourselves from this corrupt generation." Those who accepted his message were baptized, and about three thousand were added to their number that day.*

*They devoted themselves to the apostles' teaching and to the fellowship, to the breaking of bread and to prayer.*

Acts 2:37–42

I noticed that they were not commanded to be baptized in the Holy Spirit but simply to be baptized, and the Holy Spirit would be given them.

*Do not get drunk on wine, which leads to debauchery. Instead, be filled with the Spirit. Speak to one another with psalms, hymns and spiritual songs. Sing and make music in your heart to the Lord.*

Ephesians 5:18, 19

*Let the word of Christ dwell in you richly as you teach and admonish one another with all wisdom, and as you sing psalms, hymns and spiritual songs with gratitude in your hearts to God.*

Colossians 3:16

Those who follow Christ as the Son of God and Savior are called "Christians."

*And when he found him, he brought him to Antioch. So for a whole year Barnabas and Saul met with the church*

9

*and taught great numbers of people. The disciples were called Christians first at Antioch.*

Acts 11:26

*However, if you suffer as a Christian, do not be ashamed, but praise God that you bear that name.*

1 Peter 4:16

Salvation comes only through Jesus Christ. No one else has his power to save me.

*Salvation is found in no one else, for there is no other name under heaven given to men by which we must be saved.*

Acts 4:12

The very thing which makes me a Christian makes me a part of Christ's church, with the Lord adding me to it.

*And the Lord added to their number daily those who were being saved.*

Acts 2:47b

*On that day a great persecution broke out against the church at Jerusalem, and all except the apostles were scattered throughout Judea and Samaria.*

Acts 8:1b

*Keep watch over yourselves and all the flock of which the Holy Spirit has made you overseers. Be shepherds of the church of God, which he bought with his own blood.*

Acts 20:28

*All the churches of Christ send greetings.*

Romans 16:16b

*To the church of God in Corinth, to those sanctified in Christ Jesus and called to be holy.*

1 Corinthians 1:2a

*To the church of the firstborn, whose names are written in heaven.*

Hebrews 12:23a

When I became a Christian, I became a part of the body of Christ.

*The body is a unit, though it is made up of many parts; and though all its parts are many, they form one body. So it is with Christ. For we were all baptized by one Spirit into one body—whether Jews or Greeks, slave or free —and we were all given the one Spirit to drink.*

1 Corinthians 12:12–13

*Now I rejoice in what was suffered for you, and I fill up in my flesh what is still lacking in regard to Christ's afflictions, for the sake of his body, which is the church.*

Colossians 1:24

I became a citizen of the kingdom of heaven.

*And we pray this in order that you may live a life worthy of the Lord and may please him in every way: bearing fruit in every good work, growing in the knowledge of God . . . For he has rescued us from the dominion of darkness and brought us into the kingdom of the Son he loves, in whom we have redemption, the forgiveness of sins.*

Colossians 1:10–13, 14

And I became a child in the family of God.

*Although I hope to come to you soon, I am writing you these instructions so that, if I am delayed, you will know how people ought to conduct themselves in God's household, which is the church of the living God, the pillar and foundation of the truth.*

1 Timothy 3:14–15

*When Apollos wanted to go to Achaia, the brothers encouraged him and wrote to the disciples there to welcome him. On arriving, he was a great help to those who by grace had believed.*

Acts 18:27

Now that I'm a Christian, I am a part of the church of Christ, and I can benefit from Paul's instructions to Timothy:

*Do your best to present yourself to God as one approved, a workman who does not need to be ashamed and who correctly handles the word of truth.*

2 Timothy 2:15

*And how from infancy you have known the holy Scriptures, which are able to make you wise for salvation through faith in Christ Jesus.*

2 Timothy 3:15

I need to study the Bible because . . .

*All Scripture is God-breathed and is useful for teaching, rebuking, correcting and training in righteousness, so that the man of God may be thoroughly equipped for every good work.*

2 Timothy 3:16, 17

# Books of the Bible

The Bible has two main divisions:

## Old Testament

Contains 39 books, which may be grouped into five classifications

1. Law ................................ 5 books
2. History ......................... 12 books
3. Poetry ............................ 5 books
4. Major Prophets .............. 5 books
5. Minor Prophets ........... 12 books

## New Testament

Contains 27 books, which may be grouped into five classifications

1. Gospels ....................... 4 books
2. History ......................... 1 book
3. Paul's Letters ............. 13 books
4. Other Letters ............... 8 books
5. Prophecy ..................... 1 book

### Books of Law

Genesis

Exodus

Leviticus

Numbers

Deuteronomy

### Books of History

Joshua

Judges

Ruth

1 Samuel, 2 Samuel

1 Kings, 2 Kings

1 Chronicles, 2 Chronicles

Ezra

Nehemiah

Esther

### Books of Poetry

Job

### Gospels

Matthew

Mark

Luke

John

### Book of Church History

Acts

### Paul's Letters

Romans

1 Corinthians, 2 Corinthians

Galatians

Ephesians

Philippians

Colossians

1 Thessalonians, 2 Thessalonians

1 Timothy, 2 Timothy

Titus

Philemon

| (Old Testament) | (New Testament) |
| --- | --- |
| Psalms | **Other Letters** |
| Proverbs | Hebrews |
| Ecclesiastes | James |
| Song of Songs | 1 Peter, 2 Peter |
| **Books of Major Prophets** | 1 John, 2 John, 3 John |
| Isaiah | Jude |
| Jeremiah | **Book of Prophecy** |
| Lamentations | Revelation |
| Ezekiel | |
| Daniel | |
| **Books of Minor Prophets** | |
| Hosea | |
| Joel | |
| Amos | |
| Obadiah | |
| Jonah | |
| Micah | |
| Nahum | |
| Habakkuk | |
| Zephaniah | |
| Haggai | |
| Zechariah | |
| Malachi | |

A look into each of these groups will enable me to understand their relation to each other, for whom they were written, their purpose, and their contents. Then I will be able to understand them correctly.

# Old Testament

## Books of Law

The first five books are called "law" because in them we find the Law of God as given to his people through Moses. There is a great deal of history in these books but they are predominantly law and, therefore, are given that name.

We call them the "Books of Moses" because Moses wrote them. They are also called the "Pentateuch," for they are really one work with five divisions—a five-volume work by Moses.

**Genesis** is the book of beginnings of God's chosen people. Genesis begins with the creation of heaven and earth. It covers the Flood, the lives of the great fathers (Abraham, Isaac, and Jacob), their going down into Egypt, through the death of Joseph.

**Exodus** begins with the birth of Moses, the account of his training, his exile in Midian and his return to lead the Israelites out of Egypt (the Exodus). It includes the journey to Mount Sinai, the encampment there, the receiving of God's law through Moses and instructions for building the tabernacle. Exodus ends with the Israelites still camped at the foot of Mount Sinai.

**Leviticus** contains instructions for the Levites in handling the tabernacle and related ceremonies, feast days, etc. It is the "Priest's Handbook."

**Numbers** continues with the Law. It contains data concerning the number of people in the various tribes, their duties, etc., and is, therefore, sometimes called the "Census Report." Numbers also gives regulations for traveling through the wilderness. It tells of the Israelites' reaching the Promised Land after wandering in the wilderness for forty years.

**Deuteronomy** tells of the Israelites' arrival at the Jordan River after forty years of wanderings. They were ready to enter the Promised Land. But Moses had been told that he could not go into the land. So he called representatives of the twelve tribes before him and recounted their history up to that time. He repeated the law and emphasized it with a great deal of prophecy. He told the people what their dire fate would be if they departed from God's law. But he also told them of the blessings that would be theirs if they remained faithful. Deuteronomy is a collection of Moses' speeches.

## Books of History

**Joshua** records his taking Moses' place as leader of the Israelites. It describes his conquest of the land of Canaan and the settlement of the tribes in the Promised Land after conquering its inhabitants.

**Judges** continues the story of the Israelites for approximately 450 years after the settlement of Canaan. The people were governed by judges, through whom God spoke to the people. Judges covers the lives and deeds of the first twelve judges.

**Ruth** is a rural romance, picturing the condition of the common people during the violent period of the judges. It introduces into history the Moabitess, Ruth, the great-grandmother of King David, who was in the direct lineage of Christ.

**First Samuel** continues the story of God's people through the leadership of Eli and Samuel, who was the fifteenth and last judge. The Israelites called for a king.

Samuel, in obedience to God's directions, appointed Saul as the first king of Israel. This book records Israel's history through the death of Saul.

**Second Samuel** tells the history of the next king, David, who was called a "man after God's heart." Although First and Second Samuel are history through the reigns of the first two kings, it is natural that the record should be in Samuel's books for they were associated with him.

**First Kings** records the various kings of Israel from the reign of Solomon to the death of Ahab. It also explains the dividing of the kingdom into the northern kingdom, Israel, and the southern kingdom, Judah.

**Second Kings** continues the record of the kings until Israel and Judah have been captured and deported from their native lands into foreign captivity. Many of the ten tribes of Israel never returned, but the tribes of Judah and Benjamin were later restored to the Promised Land.

**First Chronicles** gives a parallel account of the same portion of history that is covered in 1 Kings.

**Second Chronicles** is simply another account of the history found in 2 Kings.

**Ezra** shows the captive Israelite people in Babylon as they begin to return to Jerusalem and rebuild it after seventy years of captivity.

**Nehemiah** gives more history of this same Period of Restoration, since Nehemiah and Ezra were contemporaries. They worked together some of the time in the reconstruction of Jerusalem and restoration of the worship of Jehovah.

**Esther** provides a glimpse into what was happening to the Jews (people of Judah) during their exile through daring experiences of a Jewish maiden, Esther, who became queen of the Persian empire. Although God's name is not found in this book, without it the Jews' history would be incomplete.

## Books of Poetry

**Job** belongs to the Patriarchal Period (or period of the great fathers) in background and outlook. Job is thought to have been contemporary with Abraham, although his experiences may have been put into its dramatic form much later by Solomon. The theme of Job is why righteous people must suffer.

**Psalms** is a collection of well-crafted poems and songs, ranging in theme from adoration of Jehovah to ballads commemorating heroic events in the history of Israel. Many of them were written by King David. They cover a long period of time, some having to do with David's shepherd days and others with experiences during the exile.

**Proverbs** is a collection of wise sayings written by King Solomon (the wisest man to ever live). It begins with an eloquent tribute to wisdom, personified as a lady who calls us to consider what is best in life. It goes through many phases of life, from domestic scenes to the marketplace.

**Ecclesiastes** is a sort of autobiography, probably written by Solomon toward the end of his life. He meditates over the meaning of life and finds that no physical or material pleasure gives permanent satisfaction. He had tried them all and knew what he was talking about.

His conclusion is that all people should remember their Creator when they are young and that to fear God and keep his commandments is the whole duty of man.

**Song of Songs,** also known as Song of Solomon, means the greatest of songs. It is believed by some to be a collection of fragments from many ancient love songs, woven together in such a way as to give a possible account of how a beautiful country maiden refused to allow the allurements of Solomon to come between her and her rustic shepherd lover. Older interpretations say the book is an allegory of the relationship between Christ and the church, but it is doubtful that the book is more than a collection of romantic verses of Solomon's writing or choosing. It probably has nothing to do with the church.

## Books of Major Prophets

A prophet was a special messenger from God. There are five of these major books and only four prophets. *Major* refers only to the books of longer length. It does not indicate importance. Minor prophets are the shorter books.

Every prophet who wrote one or more of these books can be placed in the history of Israel, which is covered by the twelve books of history. Each of these, and the minor prophecies, are to be understood only by knowing in what period of history the prophet lived and by knowing the conditions of his people at the time he prophesied to them. To see the prophets against their background is to see deep meaning in their writings and to throw much light on the history given all too briefly in some of the books of history. Let us place each of them in a historical setting in order to understand their writings.

**Isaiah** wrote during the reign of Hezekiah, king of Judah, just at the time when the fall of Jerusalem was threatened by invaders from Assyria. He wrote before the exile, but he looked beyond it to the coming of Christ the Messiah and had more to say about Christ than any other prophet. He is, therefore, sometimes called the "Messianic Prophet."

**Jeremiah** did his work a little later than Isaiah. He was most prominent at the time Jerusalem fell to the Babylonians. His message was the coming defeat of Judah and its captivity. Seeing the impossibility of its holding out against its besiegers, he advised them to surrender to save the city from complete destruction. But he was branded a traitor for his warnings that later came true.

**Lamentations** was also written by Jeremiah soon after Jerusalem fell and is a series of laments over the destruction of Jerusalem while it lay ruined and desolate.

**Ezekiel** contains the messages of God through Ezekiel, who prophesied while the Jews were in exile in Babylon.

**Daniel** is another prophet of the Exile, who foretold many events by interpreting the dreams of the Babylonian king, Nebuchadnezzar. He interpreted the meaning of the strange handwriting which appeared on the wall of Belshazzar, as well as more direct visions of things to come.

## Books of Minor Prophets

To understand these prophecies, it is necessary to know how they fit into Jewish history. The following outline of historical events divides all Old Testament events into twelve periods and identifies which Old Testament books were written during these times.

| Periods of Biblical History | Old Testament Books Covering these Periods |
|---|---|
| 1. Period before the Flood: from Creation to the Flood—4004 (a traditional date) to 2348 B.C. | Genesis |
| 2. Period after the Flood: from the Flood to the call of Abraham—2348–1921 B.C. | Genesis |
| 3. Patriarchal Age: from the call of Abraham to the sojourn in Egypt—1921–1706 B.C. | Genesis |
| 4. Egyptian Bondage: from the sojourn in Egypt to the Exodus—1706–1491 B.C. | Exodus Leviticus |
| 5. Wanderings: from the Exodus to the crossing of the Jordan River—1491–1451 B.C. | Exodus Numbers Deuteronomy |
| 6. Conquest: from the crossing of the Jordan to the settlement of the tribes—1451–1400 B.C. | Joshua |
| 7. Judges: from the settlement of the tribes to the establishment of the kingdom—1400–1050 B.C. | Judges Ruth |
| 8. The United Kingdom: from the establishment of the kingdom to the division of the kingdom—1050–931 B.C. | I Samuel, 2 Samuel I Kings I Chronicles |

| Periods of Biblical History | Old Testament Books Covering these Periods |
|---|---|
| 9. The Divided Kingdom: from the division of the kingdom to the fall of Samaria—931–722 B.C. | 2 Kings<br>2 Chronicles |
| 10. Judah Alone: from the fall of Samaria to the fall of Jerusalem—722–586 B.C. | 2 Kings<br>2 Chronicles |
| 11. Exile from the fall of Jerusalem to the fall of Babylon—586–538 B.C. | Ezra<br>Nehemiah<br>Esther |
| 12. Restoration: from the fall of Babylon to the close of the Nehemiah's career—583–432 B.C. | Ezra<br>Nehemiah<br>Esther |

Now all the prophecies may be located in those periods of history, except that Malachi was probably written after the close of Nehemiah's career. The following shows the prophets in the periods in which they lived and prophesied.

## Prophets in History

**Period of the Divided Kingdom:** Isaiah, Hosea Joel, Amos, Jonah, and Micah.

**Period of Judah Alone:** Jeremiah, Nahum, Habakkuk, and Zephaniah.

**Period of Exile:** Ezekiel, Daniel, Obadiah, and Lamentations.

**Period of Restoration:** Haggai, Zechariah, and Malachi.

A careful reading should be given to the entire Old Testament for a clearer understanding that it was all a preparation for the events recorded in the New Testament.

There are differences of opinion among the scholars concerning the dates of a few of the minor prophets. While there are some who would make a few changes in the above placement, there are other equally reputable scholars who will agree to the arrangement.

One remarkable thing is brought out: the clear truth that prophecies about the restoration of the Jews to their native land and the rebuilding of Jerusalem were all fulfilled in the return under Zerubbabel (who is told of in the book of Ezra), Ezra, and Nehemiah. All those prophecies were uttered before the restoration had been accomplished.

# New Testament

## Gospels

The books of Matthew, Mark, Luke, and John record the life of Christ. John begins his book with a "prologue" explaining that Christ was "in the beginning." All that is known authentically of Christ's life on earth, his personal ministry, is contained in these Gospels. They tell us of him from the angel Gabriel's announcement of his coming birth, through his teaching and working with the people. They tell how he was crucified, buried, raised from the dead, and ascended. They tell how he gave the apostles directions for their work after he was gone. Those directions are sometimes call The Great Commission (Matthew 28:18–19; Mark 16:15–16).

### Book of Church History

Acts is the book of history which records the apostles' activities in Jerusalem from Christ's ascension until the day of Pentecost when the church was established. Then they went as their Lord commanded, "making disciples of all nations." The book gives us the history of the church, spreading the gospel, converting individuals, and establishing congregations until around A.D. 70.

## Paul's Letters

These books are just what the title suggests, letters written by the apostle Paul to various individuals and congregations. They contain instructions for the organization of the church, the work of congregations, and for Christian living.

## Other Letters

These letters were written by persons other than Paul to individuals and congregations and contain instructions concerning the work of congregations and Christian living.

## Book of Prophecy

Revelation was written by the apostle John. It is a record of the vision he had of things that were "soon to come." It is highly figurative, containing many symbols which have been variously interpreted by different ones. Great care should be used in studying this book.

The New Testament alone teaches me how to become a Christian and how the church today is to be organized and function. In the Gospels, I learn of Christ; in Acts I learn how men and women became Christians under the teaching of the apostles who were guided by the Holy Spirit; and in Acts and in the letters I learn how congregations and individual Christians are to work and live so as to be well pleasing to the Master.

This revelation is complete and final. It is all in the New Testament. In the New Testament are instructions and guidance for my life today:

*All Scripture is God-breathed and is useful for teaching, rebuking, correcting and training in righteousness, so that the man of God may be thoroughly equipped for every good work.*　　2 Timothy 3:16–17

*Dear friends, although I was very eager to write to you about the salvation we share, I felt I had to write and urge you to contend for the faith that was once for all entrusted to the saints.*
　　　　　　　　　　　　　　　　　　Jude 3

Let us study it, every book and every chapter, so that we may obey Paul's instructions to *"study to shew thyself approved unto God, a workman that needeth not to be ashamed, rightly dividing the word of truth"* (2 Timothy 2:15, KJV).

Now that I am a Christian, I am one of the "living stones" who makes up the church which Peter writes about in 1 Peter 2:5:

*You also, like living stones, are being built into a spiritual house to be a holy priesthood, offering spiritual sacrifices acceptable to God through Jesus Christ.*

Therefore, I need to know something of the church: its worship, its organization, its work. God's magnificent wisdom is seen through the church (Ephesians 3:10–11), which is made up of the followers of Christ—those who have been saved.

*Praising God and enjoying the favor of all the people. And the Lord added to their number daily those who were being saved.*

Acts 2:47

In Acts 8:1 the people the Lord added to the original group of followers, as well as the original group, are referred to as the church.

*But Saul began to destroy the church. Going from house to house, he dragged off men and women and put them in prison.*

*Those who had been scattered preached the word wherever they went.*

Acts 8: 3–4

So it is seen that those who obey Peter's command to repent and be baptized were added by the Lord to his church. The "oneness" of the church is seen from Ephesians 4:4-6:

*There is one body and one Spirit—just as you were called to one hope when you were called—one Lord, one faith, one baptism; one God and Father of all, who is over all and through all and in all.*

*And he is the head of the body, the church; he is the beginning and the firstborn from among the dead, so that in everything he might have the supremacy.*

Colossians 1:18

The first thing I will study in this connection is worship, for that is what most people see first about the church.

# Worship of the Church

What is worship? Worship is a condition of mind, expressed through outward activities, either individually or in an assembly of people. Worship is an attitude of awe, reverence, and respect, which results in praise and honor to God. How can this praise and honor be expressed? Here are some ways the Bible gives:

## Singing

> *Speak to one another with psalms, hymns and spiritual songs. Sing and make music in your heart to the Lord.*
>
> Ephesians 5:19

> *Let the word of Christ dwell in you richly as you teach and admonish one another with all wisdom, and as you sing psalms, hymns and spiritual songs with gratitude in your hearts to God.*
>
> Colossians 3:16

> *Through Jesus, therefore, let us continually offer to God a sacrifice of praise—the fruit of lips that confess his name.*
>
> Hebrews 13:15

> *So what shall I do? I will pray with my spirit, but I will also pray with my mind; I will sing with my spirit, but I will also sing with my mind.*
>
> 1 Corinthians 14:15

From these passages it is seen that singing with the spirit and understanding honors the God who created us and saved us by his grace.

## Praying

> They devoted themselves to the apostles' teaching and to the fellowship, to the breaking of bread and to prayer.
>
> Acts 2:42

> Pray continually; give thanks in all circumstances, for this is God's will for you in Christ Jesus. ...Brothers pray for us.
>
> 1 Thessalonians 5:17–18, 25

## Teaching

> We proclaim him, admonishing and teaching everyone with all widsom, so that we may present everyone perfect in Christ.
>
> Colossians 1:28

We can bring people to Jesus, and we can help prepare other Christians for service by teaching God's Word. (See Ephesians 4:11–16)

## Communing

> They devoted themselves to the apostles' teaching and to the fellowship, to the breaking of bread and to prayer.
>
> Acts 2:42

> On the first day of the week we came together to break bread. Paul spoke to the people and, because he intended to leave the next day, kept on talking until midnight.
>
> Acts 20:7

In this we see that Christians assembled on the first day of the week to break bread (communion). Also Paul preached in that service and, by verse 36, they are praying together. (See also 1 Corinthians 11:23-29).

## Giving

> Now about the collection for God's people: Do what I told the Galatian churches to do. On the first day of every

*week, each one of you should set aside a sum of money in keeping with his income, saving it up, so that when I come no collections will have to be made.*

1 Corinthians 16:1, 2

See also 2 Corinthians 9, especially verses 6 and 7. From these I see that giving is to be done on the first day of the week, too. This shows how my giving is to be done:

1. as I have prospered,
2. as I have purposed in my heart, and
3. liberally and cheerfully.

True, it does not say "every" first day. Neither did the old law say "Remember every Sabbath day," but no one questions that every Sabbath day was to be kept holy under Moses' law. As often as it is the first day, that often will Christians assemble, if they are to follow the example of the early Christians who were taught by the apostles. Paul did not say "as seldom" as you do this but, *"For whenever you eat this bread and drink this cup, you proclaim the Lord's death until he comes"* (1 Corinthians 11:26). Our giving should not be stingy but abundant and joyous.

The regular assembly of Christians is for every Christian who can be present. It is a time of encouragement and fellowship. It's a time of joy and celebration. It's a time to praise, honor, and glorify God for his saving grace.

*Let us not give up meeting together, as some are in the habit of doing, but let us encourage one another— and all the more as you see the Day approaching.*

Hebrews 10:25

# Personal Study Notes

# Organization of the Church

Now that I'm a Christian, I will attend the assemblies of the church gladly and receive inspiration and encouragement from the joint studying of God's Word, from the communion in which I am reminded of the sacrifice that Christ made for me, and in the sweet association with my family of fellow Christians. But I want to look behind the scenes; I want to know what the New Testament teaches on how the church is organized and how it functions.

On the day of Pentecost in the year that Jesus was raised from the dead, the apostles were waiting in Jerusalem with 120 other disciples as Jesus had instructed them to do (Acts 1).

Then the power they had been promised came to them. "Peter stood up with the eleven" apostles and preached to the people, telling them the meaning of the strange things they were witnessing. His hearers were cut to the heart when they realized the enormity of their sin: *"Let all Israel be assured of this: God has made Jesus, whom you crucified, both Lord and Christ"* (Acts 2:36).

*Those who accepted his message were baptized, and about three thousand were added to their number that day.*

Acts 2:41

That's how the church began. That group of people in Jerusalem recognized the divinity of Christ and wanted to be forgiven of their sins so they might be disciples of the Lord. They received forgiveness of their sins when they accepted Christ by turning away from their former manner of life and by being baptized. Then they were added to the group of Christ's followers who were already there, mentioned in Acts 1. At this point they are not even referred to as the church. Those who accepted the Lord that day, through Peter's preaching, were thinking only of receiving forgiveness of their sins and becoming disciples of the Lord. The group is referred to in Luke's history simply as "them," and a little later as "disciples."

The group of disciples grew rapidly until it became a large number of followers of Christ (Acts 2:41; 4:4; 6:1, 7). When the great persecution came upon them after the stoning of Stephen, they were scattered and were then referred as "the church" (Acts 8:1).

## Elders and Deacons

The first need for organization in the church, in addition to the leadership and teaching of the apostles themselves, arose in Jerusalem. The Grecian disciples complained that their widows were being neglected in the daily distribution of food (Acts 6:1). To administer the work, seven men were selected from among the disciples and were placed in charge of the work (Acts 6:3). Those seven men are not called "deacons" in the text, but they are often referred to as the deacons of the Jerusalem church. (The word *deacon* simply means "servant.")

Further growth and development of the church later led to the appointing of elders. By the time of the meeting in Jerusalem (Acts 15) there were elders. Notice verses 2, 4, 6, 22, and 23. They were taking a prominent part, along with the apostles, in the work of the church.

Paul's famous speech to the elders of the church of Ephesus is found in Acts 20. From this chapter several important principles are learned.

The qualifications for elders and deacons are found in 1 Timothy 3 and Titus 1, as well as scattered passages elsewhere which emphasize various duties and characteristics of elders.

In these passages organization of the church in the New Testament is pictured. There were congregations of "disciples" or "brothers" (1 Corinthians 1:10, 26; Acts 15:33-36) who were called "Christians," first at Antioch (Acts 11:26), and were sometimes referred to as "saints" as in Ephesians 1:1.

In these congregations there were elders and deacons. The elders had oversight of the congregation (1 Peter 5:1-3), and the deacons ministered as its servants.

Each congregation had its elders (overseers) and was independent of all other congregations. There is no hint in the New Testament that any congregation, nor any elder in it, had any control whatsoever of any other congregation. There was absolute independence of congregations; each taking care of its own affairs under the supervision of its own elders, with the ministries of its deacons.

These men who had the oversight of the congregation were called "overseers." Referring to them as "elders" indicates that they were supposed to be mature men who were experienced. They were also called "pastors," to signify their duty of feeding the flock. All these names were applied to the same group of men, each title conveying a different characteristic or responsibility of these men. Observe from the above facts these important considerations:

1. The overseers or elders were in the plural over one congregation, not a number of congregations under one overseer.
2. Elders are to be shepherds to the members, serving as leaders and examples.
3. Elders are men of spiritual maturity. They are chosen by a congregation from among themselves, according to the qualifications in the Bible. These men serve the congregation as long as the congregation wants them to continue. Under the elders' guidance, the entire church is responsible to Christ, who is its only head.

## Minister

The minister's (or evangelist's) primary responsibility is to preach the Word of God for the congregation. It is his privilege to encourage and lift up the church with his spiritual gift of preaching. It is also his privilege to preach and teach the good news of Jesus Christ to the lost people who hear him.

The New Testament church is not complicated in its organization. It is simple and effective.

The New Testament scriptures must remain the authoritative guide for my worship, work, and church organizational structure as I lose my own identity in the name and body of Christ, the church. Unity is the constant goal of New Testament Christians as we relate to each other and try to determine God's purposes and goals for us. Paul pleads:

> *I appeal to you, brothers, in the name of our Lord Jesus Christ, that all of you agree with one another so that there may be no divisions among you and that you may be perfectly united in mind and thought.*

1 Corinthians 1:10

To progress toward this unity or "oneness" (a goal not merely for the many differing churches, but one to be set within each congregation), I want to make a proper response to the Bible. Individual Christians and Christians collectively need to ask these two questions: What *did* the Bible writer say? (Or, What was the message for the people of his day?) and What *does* the Bible writer say? (Or, What message does he have for me today?) Methods change with changing times, but the real message of the inspired writer does not change. Methods of communication change, but the message to be communicated does not change.

When Paul admonished Timothy to "correctly handle the word of truth" (2 Timothy 2:15), he was telling him to find out what the writer's true message was and is.

It should be my sincerest desire always to learn the true meaning of a scripture and make the right response to it.

# Personal Study Notes

# Work of the Church

After studying the worship and organization of the church, the question naturally arises, organized for what? The church is under the oversight of the elders, who are to see that no false doctrine is taught to the Christians and that no unauthorized practice is carried on by them.

> *Keep watch over yourselves and all the flock of which the Holy Spirit has made you overseers. Be shepherds of the church of God, which he bought with his own blood. I know that after I leave, savage wolves will come in among you and will not spare the flock. Even from your own number men will arise and distort the truth in order to draw away disciples after them.*
> Acts 20:28-30

(Also see Titus 1:7-10; 1 Peter 5:1-9)

But is the church to care only for its members? Is it only to perpetuate itself as a "society of the contented?" Emphatically, no! The church is to be like Christ . . .

> *Who gave himself for us to redeem us from all wickedness and to purify for himself a people that are his very own, eager to do what is good.*
> Titus 2:14

> *So that the man of God may be thoroughly equipped for every good work.*
> 2 Timothy 3:17

The church is the only institution through which God makes known to the world his purpose for humanity:

*His intent was that now, through the church, the manifold wisdom of God should be made known to the rulers and authorities in the heavenly realms, according to his eternal purpose which he accomplished in Christ Jesus our Lord.*

Ephesians 3:10, 11

The church is supposed to . . .

*Preach the Word; be prepared in season and out of season; correct, rebuke and encourage—with great patience and careful instruction.*

2 Timothy 4:2

(See also Matthew 28:19, 20; 1 Thessalonians 1:6–8; 2 Timothy 3:1–4).

No congregation is really following the New Testament pattern unless it shares the message of salvation in its own community and beyond as it has opportunity. For a church to be like the first-century church, it must be mission minded. It must be doing evangelistic work, at home in its own community and nearby communities, and by sending or helping to send people who will carry the good news of salvation to the world.

Now that I'm a Christian, I want to do my part so that the local church, of which I am a part, can reach out to the lost.

But that's not all. Preaching from the pulpit on Sunday mornings is not all that a congregation needs to be interested in. Not only the preacher, but every individual Christian can influence his associates in the right direction and try to lead them to become Christians, too. In the early days of the church, Christians shared the good news about Jesus personally.

*On that day a great persecution broke out against the church at Jerusalem, and all except the apostles were scattered throughout Judea and Samaria. Godly men buried Stephen and mourned deeply for him. But Saul began to destroy the church. Going from house to house, he dragged off men and women and put them in prison.*

*Those who had been scattered preached the word wherever they went.*

Acts 8:1-4

There is no such distinction in the New Testament as "clergy" and "laity." Every Christian has a gift to use in the church.

Some can do the public preaching, such as Paul, Timothy, Titus, Apollos, and others. Some can teach classes (Ephesians 4:11-14). Some can sing, some can encourage, some can serve in other ways. We are to do whatever we can in whatever place we find ourselves.

*Therefore, as we have opportunity, let us do good to all people, especially to those who belong to the family of believers.*

Galatians 6:10

*Religion that God our Father accepts as pure and faultless is this: to look after orphans and widows in their distress and to keep oneself from being polluted by the world.*

James 1:27

*The disciples, each according to his ability, decided to provide help for the brothers living in Judea. This they did, sending their gift to the elders by Barnabas and Saul.*

Acts 11:29, 30

*(Also see Romans 12:4-13; Galatians 6:10; Ephesians 4:28; 1 Timothy 6:17-19).*

The work of the church is, first of all, to preach the gospel, which can be done in many different ways by

Christians with many different gifts. While that is being done, each Christian lives a life of purity and godliness, helping his neighbors in any way that he can. The whole body of Christians, the church in a particular place, will also do many things collectively which cannot be accomplished by individuals.

# Christian Living

Now that I'm a Christian, I want to know how I should conduct myself in my various personal relationships and activities. I have reviewed how I became a Christian. I have surveyed the divisions of the Bible, both to comprehend it and for my guidance. I have studied the church as a group of Christians in a community.

Now, I need to study further to find instructions and guidance for my private and personal life. Here are just a few highlights covering broad principles which will serve as a beginning for a more thorough study through the years.

I have learned already that God's grace through my faith in Christ prompts me to live as holy and righteously as I can. In addition to the other passages on the subject which I have considered, this is emphasized by Peter (2 Peter 1:3-11).

Here are qualities I will try to develop in my everyday living: (1) my activities will be virtuous; (2) I will always be striving for more knowledge; (3) I will develop self-control; (4) I will learn patience; (5) godliness will be my goal; (6) I will try to show kindness to all; (7) and in all things I will try to show a spirit of love (1 Corinthians 13). Not all these qualities can be learned overnight. It may take a long time to attain great improvement, but the Christian life is described as a race, a battle, and as growth. So, I will try to grow day by day to be more like my Master until, after some years, all who know me may see the sincerity and reality of my Christianity.

> *But grow in the grace and knowledge of our Lord and Savior Jesus Christ.*
>
> 2 Peter 3:18

Some passages list specific sins for me to avoid. These things are inherently sinful everywhere, in every age.

**Galatians 5:9-21:** being sexually unfaithful, not being pure, taking part in sexual sins, worshiping false gods, doing witchcraft, hating, making trouble, being jealous, being angry, being selfish, making people angry with each other, causing divisions among people, having envy, being drunk, having wild and wasteful parties, and doing other things like this.

**1 Corinthians 5:11; 6:9:** taking part in sexual sin, being selfish, worshiping idols, lying about others, getting drunk, or cheating people.

**Colossians 3:5-9:** sexual sinning, doing evil, letting evil thoughts control me, wanting things that are evil, always selfishly wanting more and more, living to serve a false god, showing anger and having a bad temper, doing or saying things to hurt others, using evil words when I talk, and lying.

**2 Timothy 3:1-5:** loving myself too much, loving money, bragging, having too much pride, saying evil things against others, disobeying my parents, not being thankful, not being the kind of person God wants, not having love for others, refusing to forgive others, speaking bad things, not having self-control, being cruel, hating what is good, turning against friends, doing foolish things without thinking, being conceited, loving pleasure and not loving God.

**Revelation 22:15:** doing evil magic, sinning sexually, being a murderer, worshiping idols, loving lies, and telling lies.

These things are universally wrong. I will try hard not to allow any of them to creep into my thinking and living.

It is important for me to know that such things as lying, disobedience to parents, speaking evil, and envying are among the things which will keep me out of God's favor. Some things which are lightly passed over in our modern life cannot be tolerated in the life of a Christian. Notice how prominent in these lists are drunkenness, sexual sin, and abusive language.

Far reaching in its application is Paul's instruction to the Thessalonians: "Avoid every kind of evil" (1 Thessalonians 5:22).

And yet, I know that every living person sins:

*As it is written: "There is no one righteous, not even one. . . For all have sinned and fall short of the glory of God".*
Romans 3:10, 23

That means I'm a sinner, too. But as a Christian, I have been saved by God's grace.

*What shall we say, then? Shall we go on sinning so that grace may increase? By no means! We died to sin; how can we live in it any longer? . . . Therefore do not let sin reign . . . but rather offer yourselves to God, as those who have been brought from death to life; and offer the parts of your body to him as instruments of righteousness.*

Romans 6:1, 2, 12a, 13b

I have learned that when I sin as a Christian, I need to confess my sins, and I'll be forgiven.

*If we claim to be without sin, we deceive ourselves and the truth is not in us. If we confess our sins, he is faithful and just and will forgive us our sins and purify us from all unrighteousness.*

1 John 1:8, 9

In addition to these negative things, things which are to be left out, there are some positive things which must be *grown into* my life.

Broadly speaking, the New Testament is not a book of rules. It is a book of principles. Remember that the New Testament is a book written for all succeeding ages. So it cannot list certain things which are peculiar to one country or one age, for that would be meaningless to other people in other centuries or other countries.

The wisdom of the Bible is that it does not deal in specific items that are transitory. It deals with principles I must understand; then, from those principles, I must chart my course in any community in any social or economic order, such as the principles of honesty, sobriety, kindness, and helpfulness.

Here are the principles by which God will shape my living:

*For the grace of God that brings salvation has appeared to all men. It teaches us to say "No" to*

*ungodliness and worldly passions, and to live self-controlled, upright and godly lives in this present age.*
Titus 2:11, 12

*Don't you know that you yourselves are God's temple and that God's Spirit lives in you? If anyone destroys God's temple, God will destroy him; for God's temple is sacred, and you are that temple.*
1 Corinthians 3:16, 17

*Therefore, as we have opportunity, let us do good to all people, especially to those who belong to the family of believers.*
Galatians 6:10

The positive approach study also includes the following passages:

*Therefore, if anyone is in Christ, he is a new creation; the old has gone, the new has come!*
2 Corinthians 5:17

*Neither circumcision nor uncircumcision means anything; what counts is a new creation.*
Galatians 6:15

(See also Romans 14:15-17, 21; Ephesians 4:17-25;<br>Philippians 2:12-18; 4:4-9; 1 John 2:12-17)

As a new creature, a "new self," I will not live against God and do evil things the world wants to do, but live on earth now in a wise and right way—a way that shows that we serve God out of gratitude for His saving grace (Titus 2:11, 12). I will be careful not to cause someone to be offended by what I do (Romans 14:21).

*Do everything without complaining or arguing, so that you may become blameless and pure, children of God without fault in a crooked and depraved generation, in which you shine like stars in the universe.*

Philippians 2:14, 15

*For this very reason, make every effort to add to your faith goodness; and to goodness, knowledge; and to knowledge, self-control; and to self-control, perseverance; and to perseverance, godliness; and to godliness, brotherly kindness; and to brotherly kindness, love. For if you possess these qualities in increasing measure, they will keep you from being ineffective and unproductive in your knowledge of our Lord Jesus Christ.*

2 Peter 1:5-8

*But the fruit of the Spirit is love, joy, peace, patience, kindness, goodness, faithfulness, gentleness and self-control. Against such things there is no law.*

Galatians 5:22–23

*He who has been stealing must steal no longer, but must work, doing something useful with his own hands, that he may have something to share with those in need.*

Ephesians 4:28

*Always giving thanks to God the Father for everything, in the name of our Lord Jesus Christ.*

Ephesians 5:20

All the letters may be considered instructions for Christian living. And living a Christian life brings great rewards.

*To those who by persistence in doing good seek glory, honor and immortality, he will give eternal life.*

Romans 2:7

*And into an inheritance that can never perish, spoil or fade—kept in heaven for you.*

1 Peter 1:4

The Christian life in daily association with other people is an attitude of mind and heart. It is an attitude toward life and my fellows. It is a matter of spirituality, my having the same spirit that motivated Christ:

*You, however, are controlled not by the sinful nature but by the Spirit, if the Spirit of God lives in you. And if anyone does not have the Spirit of Christ, he does not belong to Christ.*

Romans 8:9

Also, every business transaction of professional practice should be measured by these standards, and every activity of social or recreational character should be judged by the following tests:

1. Is the activity questionable in my own mind?
2. Does it destroy my identity as a Christian?
3. Does it cause someone else to sin?
4. Is it destructive to my body?
5. Does it conflict with my life as a Christian?
6. Does it weaken my influence with others?

*Do not love the world or anything in the world. If anyone loves the world, the love of the Father is not in him. For everything in the world—the cravings of sinful man, the lust of his eyes and the boasting of what he has and does—comes not from the Father but from the world. The world and its desires pass away, but the man who does the will of God lives forever.*

1 John 2:15-17

*And the God of all grace, who called you to his eternal glory in Christ, after you have suffered a little while, will himself restore you and make you strong, firm and steadfast. To him be the power for ever and ever. Amen.*

1 Peter 5:10, 11

*In all these things we are more than conquerors through him who loved us. For I am convinced that neither death nor life, neither angels nor demons, neither the present nor the future, nor any powers, neither height nor depth, nor anything else in all creation, will be able to separate us from the love of God that is in Christ Jesus our Lord.*

Romans 8:37-39

*Welcome to the family of God.*